ASSIM ALHAKEEM

FEAR AND HOPE IN ALLAH
HOW TO BALANCE?

TRANSCRIBED AND ADAPTED FROM
"FEAR AND HOPE IN ALLAH: HOW TO BALANCE?" BY ASSIM ALHAKEEM

Published by:

Unit No. E-10-5, Jalan SS 15/4G, Subang Square,
47500 Subang Jaya, Selangor, Malaysia
+603-5612-2407 (office) / +6017-399-7411 (mobile)
info@tertib.press
www.tertib.press
@tertibpress (Facebook & Instagram)

Author	:	Assim Alhakeem
Transcriber & Editor	:	Arisha Mohd Affendy
Proofreader	:	Nadiah Aslam
Cover designer	:	Abdul Adzim Md Daim
Typesetter	:	Abdul Adzim Md Daim

FEAR AND HOPE IN ALLAH: HOW TO BALANCE?

First Edition: May 2024

Perpustakaan Negara Malaysia

Cataloguing-in-Publication Data

A catalogue record for this book is available from the National Library of Malaysia

ISBN: 978-967-2844-33-4 (hardback)

Copyright © Assim Alhakeem 2024

All rights reserved.
No part of this publication may be reproduced, distributed, or transmitted in any form or by any means, including photocopying, recording, or other electronic or mechanical methods, without the prior written permission of Tertib Publishing.
Printed in Malaysia.

Contents

PREFACE 1
INTRODUCTION 3
FEAR 5
   FEAR OF ALLAH 6
   THE STATION OF FEAR (*KHAWF*) 9
   TYPES OF FEAR 16
   STAGE OF FEAR IN THE LENS OF THE PROPHET AND HIS *ṢAḤABAH* 25
   BENEFITS OF HAVING FEAR OF ALLAH 31
HOPE 37
   HOPE IN ALLAH 38
   AR-RAJA' AND *TAMANNI* (BEING HOPEFUL VS BEING WISHFUL) 40
   ATTAINING *AR-RAJA'* 42
   BENEFITS OF HAVING HOPE IN ALLAH 47
   BALANCING *AL-KHAWF WA RAJA'* 49
   DISTINGUISHING MOMENTS OF FLUCTUATING HOPE AND FEAR 52

"By My might, I will never combine in My servant two fears or two securities. If he feared Me in the world, I will make him safe on the Day of Resurrection. If he felt secure from Me in the world, I will make him fearful on the Day of Resurrection."

(Ṣaḥiḥ ibn Hibban 640)

"...Indeed, they used to hasten to good deeds and supplicate Us in hope and fear, and they were to Us humbly submissive."

(al-Anbiya', 21:90)

Preface

All praise be to Allah, the One who is loved, hoped and feared, and may the praise and peace of Allah be upon His Messenger and his family and followers. This book was originally a lecture that I was blessed to give in Perlis, Malaysia in 2023.

The *salaf* (righteous predecessors) said: "The *iman* of the believer is like a bird where the love of Allah is the head and fear and hope are the wings. If one doesn't love Allah, the head of the bird is not found and there can't be any *iman* existing. And if one of the wings of the bird is missing or weaker than the other wing, the bird will eventually fall and fail to fly properly."

Such a balance of fearing Allah and hoping for the best while loving Him wholeheartedly is the only way to maintain *iman* in the hearts.

However, this is a fine line a believer is asked to walk on while balancing the fear and hope in Allah. This is so that he wouldn't go astray as many deviant sects have before us.

The *khawarij* and the *murjiah* are two sides of the same coin, though how ironically this may sound. They both believe that *iman* is one whole unit that cannot increase or decrease. The *khawarij* believed that the fear of Allah must dominate everything else. They also believe that the one who commits a major sin is not a believer; instead, he is a *kafir* and is destined to hell for eternity.

Al-Murji'ah believed that the hope in Allah must overwhelm everything. They also believed that *iman* is one unit; that no matter what sin one commits—whether major or minor—his *iman* is intact and not affected.

Ahlu sunnah wal jama'ah were the luckiest of all for following the Qur'an and sunnah with the understanding of the three favourite generations and having the right balance between fear and hope in Allah. They said that *iman* increases with good deeds and decreases with sins.

May Allah make us among those who attain full *iman* and manage the right balance.

Assim Luqman Alhakeem

Introduction

The topic *al-Khawf wa-Raja'*—fear and hope in Allah—is not for entertainment; it is related to *'aqidah*, the most important aspect of life. Unfortunately, many of us fail to recognise that our *'aqidah* determines our success or failure. The Messengers of Allah fought for *'aqidah* and not for wealth, property, or land. People oppose us for our beliefs displayed by our *'aqidah*. Therefore, a significant aspect of our *'aqidah* is *al-Khawf wa-Raja'*—the fear of Allah and hope in Allah *subḥānahu wa ta'ala*.

This is explicitly stated in the Qur'an. Anyone who reads the Qur'an or claims to be a Muslim will find this mentioned clearly, let alone in the sunnah. However, the Qur'an is the criterion that nobody disputes, not even the people of *bid'ah*.

What does Allah say about this topic? In the Qur'an, Allah states:

فَٱسْتَجَبْنَا لَهُۥ وَوَهَبْنَا لَهُۥ يَحْيَىٰ وَأَصْلَحْنَا لَهُۥ زَوْجَهُۥٓ ۚ إِنَّهُمْ كَانُوا۟ يُسَٰرِعُونَ فِى ٱلْخَيْرَٰتِ وَيَدْعُونَنَا رَغَبًا وَرَهَبًا ۖ وَكَانُوا۟ لَنَا خَٰشِعِينَ ۝٩٠

"So We responded to him, and We gave to him John, and amended for him his wife. Indeed, they used to hasten to good deeds and supplicate Us **in hope and fear,** and they were to Us humbly submissive."

(al-Anbiya', 21:90)

"In hope and fear" they supplicated. The Messengers of Allah used to supplicate to Allah in hope and fear. Hence, to understand how to balance between these two, we must first comprehend the meanings of fear and hope.

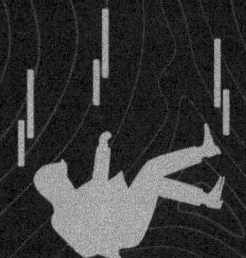

FEAR OF ALLAH

What is Fear?

Fear linguistically is to expect something bad to happen. In general, fear is when we anticipate something negative or fear of missing out on something we love and desire due to speculation. There is a sign that resonates with that intuition, and it is the trembling of the heart, unable to remain steady. This is what fear usually entails—it is the opposite of feeling secure. Security is about feeling safe and sound, without fear.

The fear of Allah (Glory be to Him, the Exalted) is a characteristic of the believers. It is the attitude of those who are knowledgeable about Allah. These people are mentioned in the Qur'an:

$$\text{إِنَّمَا يَخْشَى ٱللَّهَ مِنْ عِبَادِهِ ٱلْعُلَمَٰٓؤُاْ} \ldots \text{۝}$$

"Verily only those amongst Allah's servants that fears Allah the most are the scholars"

(Faṭir, 35:28)

Hence, Allah has limited true knowledge to those who fear Him the most. The fear of Allah is an indication of the purity of the soul and the sincerity of the heart.

It is one of the most important tasks in our religion because it has serious consequences. When we fear Allah the Almighty, it motivates us to perform good deeds and protects us from committing sins. Hence, fear holds great importance in Islam.

THE STATION OF FEAR (*KHAWF*)

The Station of Fear (*Khawf*)

Ibn Qayyum once emphasised that the *manzilah* (stage) of fear is the highest and most significant in Islam. It profoundly benefits our hearts and is *farḍ* (obligatory) for every individual. Allah has clearly instructed in the Qur'an:

> ...فَلَا تَخَافُوهُمْ وَخَافُونِ إِن كُنتُم مُّؤْمِنِينَ ۝

"...So fear them not, but **fear Me,** if you are [indeed] believers."

(Ali-'Imran, 3:175)

This indicates that a true sign of being a real *mu'min* (believer) entails fearing Allah. Without this fear, one cannot be considered a believer.

Moreover, Allah describes the messengers as *munzirin* (warners). They came to warn us. When we are warned, fear naturally arises. They warned us of Allah's punishment, so we fear Him. They warned us of the torment of hell, so we fear its flames. They warned us of the Day of Judgement, so we fear being held accountable for our actions. Thus, it is crucial to harbour this fear. Allah praises those who possess this fear in the Qur'an:

إِنَّ ٱلَّذِينَ هُم مِّنْ خَشْيَةِ رَبِّهِم مُّشْفِقُونَ ﴿٥٧﴾ وَٱلَّذِينَ هُم بِـَٔايَٰتِ رَبِّهِمْ يُؤْمِنُونَ ﴿٥٨﴾ وَٱلَّذِينَ هُم بِرَبِّهِمْ لَا يُشْرِكُونَ ﴿٥٩﴾ وَٱلَّذِينَ يُؤْتُونَ مَآ ءَاتَوا۟ وَّقُلُوبُهُمْ وَجِلَةٌ أَنَّهُمْ إِلَىٰ رَبِّهِمْ رَٰجِعُونَ ﴿٦٠﴾ أُو۟لَٰٓئِكَ يُسَٰرِعُونَ فِى ٱلْخَيْرَٰتِ وَهُمْ لَهَا سَٰبِقُونَ ﴿٦١﴾

"Indeed, they who are apprehensive from fear of their Lord. And they who believe in the signs of their Lord. And they who do not associate anything with their Lord. And they who give what they give while their hearts are fearful because they will be returning to their Lord—It is those who hasten to good deeds, and they outstrip [others] therein."

(al-Mu'minun, 23:57-61)

Reflect on these beautiful descriptions in this verse.

Mother 'A'isyah, the wife of the Prophet (praise and peace of Allah be upon him) said, "I asked the Messenger of Allah (praise and peace of Allah be upon him) about this *ayah*: And those who give that which they give with their hearts full of fear... (23:60)" 'A'isyah said: "Are they those who drink intoxicants and steal?" He said: "No, O' daughter of Aṣ-Ṣiddiq. They are those who fast, perform *ṣalah*, give charity while they fear that their Lord will not accept it from them: It is these who hasten to do good deeds, and they are the foremost of them (23:61)."

(Jamiʿ at-Tirmidhi 3175)

These verses and hadith depict individuals who, despite engaging in many good deeds, still maintain a sense of fear and humility before Allah. Do we resemble them? Do we perform acts of worship like fasting, praying, and giving charity, all while feeling afraid that Allah may not accept it from us? Or are we boasting about our good deeds and confirming our seats in Paradise and taking it for granted? Unfortunately, many of us don't feel any fear when we commit sins.

Some of us, upon completing the Qur'an perhaps once every three or four years, feel a sense of pride—even though we don't even know if Allah has accepted it from us or not. Some after performing *hajj* or *'umrah*, and returning with the expectation of leading righteous lives still persist in committing sins. When questioned about their actions, they respond, "I have accumulated good deeds. I performed *hajj*. I completed *'umrah*, so I have earned 'credits' that would entitle me to commit such small sins." So, they believe and think deep down like this even if they don't verbally dare to say it! My friend, this is not a mobile phone where you can simply top up your balance! You are dealing with Allah and you must fear Him.

If you pray, for instance, three hours of *tahajjud* and then boast about it exclaiming, "I prayed three hours of *tahajjud*. I am a renowned scholar and I have done lots of good deeds, so I have credits. And thanks to my credits I can do whatever I want." NO. This is totally wrong and dangerous! This attitude is a clear indication that you are delusional and misguided. Instead, you must feel humbled and small before Allah. You should fear that Allah may not accept your deeds instead of boasting about them as if you guarantee that Allah has accepted them. This fear drives you to perform more deeds sincerely and in a better way for His sake.

Doing something good, such as giving a hundred euros to a poor person, and afterwards feeling a sense of satisfaction is not wrong by itself, however, can you be certain that Allah accepted your deed? Some may argue, "Of course, it is accepted. I did it for Allah, so Allah will accept it." NO! You must be fearful that Allah may not accept it. This is how the righteous perceive their actions. They fear that despite their efforts, their deeds may not be accepted by Allah. This fear differentiates the righteous from the hypocrites.

Al-Ḥasan al-Baṣri (may Allah's mercy be upon him) commented on the above verses and hadiths. He noted that the righteous perform good deeds with their utmost effort while harbouring a fear that Allah may reject them. In essence, believers combine good deeds with the fear of Allah. He further commented that hypocrites, on the other hand, combined sin with feeling safe from Allah's wrath and punishment. Unfortunately, this reflects the state of many of us today. Al-Ḥasan commented on this:

> "By Allah, they (the Companions) obeyed Him and exerted themselves, yet they feared their deeds might be rejected. A believer combines righteousness with fear in his heart, whereas a hypocrite combines evil with impunity."
>
> (Madarij as-Salikin)

Fear that is genuine and praised is what prevents us from sinning. This is what Allah wants from us—to possess this fear. Allah wants us to fear having our deeds rejected. He wants us to fear Him (Glory be to Him, the Exalted) so that we become more sincere. He (Glory be to Him, the Exalted) wants us to have this fear to deter us from indulging in sins and hypocrisy.

When I inquired of some individuals, "Why don't you pray *fajr* in the *masjid*? The *masjid* is just next door." They respond, "The bed is cosy, Shaykh. The air-conditioner is cold, and I feel like sleeping."

Does such individuals have any fear of Allah or His wrath? Of course not because if he knew what awaits him in his grave and on the Day of Judgement for sleeping over a *fard* prayer, he would have been sleepless and awake all night long! Fear should motivate you to leave your bed and go to the *masjid*. Fear should prompt you to turn off the music when it plays in the car. Fear should lead you to cancel your Netflix and Showtime subscriptions. Fear should urge you to abandon all sinful activities. This is the true and genuine fear of Allah. Fear actually manifests in several categories comprising four types which we will discuss in the next chapter.

TYPES OF FEAR

Types of Fear

Mandatory Fear

The first type of fear that we will discuss is the mandatory fear. Mandatory fear is the fear that compels us to fulfil our obligations and avoid haram. Possessing this fear leads one to *Jannah*, as it prevents us from straying into the path that leads to hell. This fear is the bare minimum required, but there exists a superior form of fear known as the recommended fear.

Recommended Fear

This is a more refined form of fear that we should all strive to cultivate. It motivates us to engage in additional acts of *ʿibadah* and good deeds. While we may have fulfilled our obligatory duties, the question remains: Have we performed the sunnah? Allah has made five prayers mandatory per day, but the sunnah prayers elevates us to a higher level. The sunnah prayers help build our house in *Jannah*. Thus, the recommended fear is a fear that gives us an edge and encourages us to observe the sunnah as well. For instance, we fast every Ramadan, but if we also fast every Monday and Thursday, Allah would review our deeds on those days and approve them.

> Narrated from Abu Qatadah al-Ansari (may Allah be pleased with him) that the Messenger of Allah (praise and peace of Allah be upon him) was asked about fasting on Mondays and he said: "On (that day) I was born and on it Revelation came down to me."
>
> (Ṣaḥīḥ Muslim 1162)

Fear of Incompetence

This is the third type of fear, often experienced by those who are lazy and lethargic. This fear arises when we listen to reminders about our faith. These reminders act like a whip, causing temporary discomfort that fades after a day or two, leading us to forget the lesson. Therefore, we need another whip, followed by a third and so on as constant reminders to keep us on the right path. These reminders of fearing Allah, along with Islamic gatherings and events we attend to soften our hearts and deepen our understanding of our religion, serve as these metaphorical whips. In these moments, we experience this fear of incompetence, where we fear Allah, feel remorse, shed tears, and strive to do our best. However, as soon as the discomfort subsides, we often revert to our old habits.

This fear is beneficial because, although it is temporary, it can sometimes extend for a while, even up to a week. For example, attending the weekly *Khutbatul jumu'ah*—Friday sermon and prayers is a beautiful practice that recharges our "batteries" for the entire week. And just before this energy depletes, we attend the next Friday sermon and prayers, recharging ourselves once again.

Prohibited Fear

The fourth type of fear is the prohibited fear—the fear of *al-Khawarij*, which is an excessive fear that leads us to despair. It is the fear that makes us believe that Allah will not forgive us, and that no matter what we do, Allah will put us in hell.

Shaytan often exploits this fear. He approaches us through the door of fearing Allah, a door that is already open. However, *shaytan* pushes this door open to such an extent that we cannot close it. He then convinces us that there is no hope for us.

For instance, consider someone who is so afraid of Allah that they recite the *shahadah* fifty times a day. When asked why, they might say, "I smiled at something someone said, so I committed a *shirk*. I thought negatively about the Prophet (praise and peace of Allah be upon him), so I committed *kufr*. Therefore, I recite the *shahadah* fifty times a day." This person also performs *ghusl* five to ten times a day to embrace Islam. However, after two to three weeks, they despair of Allah's mercy. They continually say that Allah will not forgive them. And then *shaytan* comes and whispers to them, "Yes, Allah will not forgive you. So, what can you do now? There is no hope for you as you are inevitably going to hell! You might as well abandon your *salah* as there is no use of it!"

In my counselling sessions, I often meet brothers and sisters who do not pray, fast, or believe in Islam. Yet, they come to me in tears like babies, saying, "I don't want to go to hell." And I will say to them, "Don't cry *akhi*, you're already in Hell." This is called shock therapy. It's a harsh reality check that they need. If they claim to fear Allah but do not pray, then their fear is not genuine. If we truly feared Allah, we would definitely do what He commanded us to do which includes by default to pray on time.

Some people even have excessive fear of death, which is also a form of negative fear. I once met a man who was consumed by this fear. He was absolutely terrified, and looked like a pale chicken. He said, "I have this fear of death. For years, I have been restless. My wife has divorced me, I've lost my job and half of my weight Shaykh. And for the past four weeks, I cannot take a shower and I do not pray."

When I asked him how long he had been living in fear, he said, "Three years." I then asked him, "Did you die?" He replied, "Of course not." So I said, "If you didn't die in three years, what would happen if you lived like this for another fifteen years and still don't die? Are you going to live in fear for another fifteen years?"

This fear is a sign of weak *'aqidah*, and I told the brother about this. He said, "Come on Shaykh, what do you mean by weak *'aqidah*?" I asked him, "Do you know the six pillars of *iman*?" He listed the five pillars of Islam, a common mistake among many Muslims who confuse the pillars of Islam with the pillars of *iman*.

I asked him again, "Do you know the six pillars of *iman*? Do you believe in Allah? Do you believe in the Last Day—the Day of Judgement?" He said, "Yes." I asked, "Do you believe in pre-destiny and the divine decree? Do you believe that you will die on a specific day?" He said, "Yes." So I asked him, "Then why are you afraid? Look at you, you have lost everything for the past three years. If you have *iman*, you should go and work on improving yourself."

Hence this is the fourth type of fear—the **prohibited fear**. In essence, it is a negative fear that indicates a lack of *iman*. Let me give another example. A sister once told me, "Shaykh, I don't want to get married because I'm afraid to get pregnant." I said to her, "So? All women have been getting pregnant since Ḥawa' (peace be upon her). The sister replied and said, "Yes, but I'm afraid that my child will grow up in this dangerous environment filled with LGBTQ, car accidents and more." So I replied: "Sister, if you had true *iman*, trust and *tawakkul* in Allah—all of these things would not be worrying you. This is *shayṭan* messing up with your head! Imagine if you cascaded the same analogy over preparing food when you are hungry and started thinking: What if a fire started in the kitchen? What if a gas explosion happens in the kitchen while I'm cooking? What if I choke and suffocate while eating? When you have all these thoughts running in your head, you will end up never preparing food for yourself and you will die out of starvation!"

In addition, we can divide the fears into another division as well. We can categorise it into two, whereby there is the natural fear and the "secret fear" which is a form of worship.

People come to me and say, "Shaykh, I have committed *shirk* because I'm afraid of my boss, I'm afraid of the dark", or they may say "I'm afraid of my wife." This is happening all the time. Such people get anxiety and panic attacks because they fail to identify what is natural fear from what is not. Someone once asked me on "Ask Zad," "Shaykh I was praying and a lion came to attack me.

Should I continue my prayer?" So I answered, "If you could keep and preserve your *wuḍu'* in such circumstances, then continue!" If a lion comes, our *wuḍu'* would most likely break due to our fear of such a lion and the only natural thing to do would be to run! This is natural fear and it has nothing to do with *shirk*.

Sometimes, people struggle to differentiate between the fear of Allah and the fear of creatures. Even Musa (praise and peace of Allah be upon him) in the Qur'an was described as fearing Pharaoh and being afraid when his staff turned into a snake. Allah says:

فَأَوْجَسَ فِى نَفْسِهِۦ خِيفَةً مُّوسَىٰ ۝ قُلْنَا لَا تَخَفْ إِنَّكَ أَنتَ ٱلْأَعْلَىٰ ۝

"And he sensed within himself apprehension, did Moses. We [i.e., Allah] said, 'Fear not. Indeed, it is you who are superior.'"

(Ṭaha, 20:67-68)

These are natural fears. However, the fear that we should direct our attention to is the fear of Allah and this is the type of fear that must not be directed to anyone other than Allah.

If we fear someone or something as we fear Allah, while revering and praising them, then this is *shirk*. For example, if we fear the *jinn* or a deceased person while revering them and having submissiveness towards them as we do to Allah, then it is *shirk*.

Those who commit *shirk*, if we were to ask them to swear by Allah that they did not do something or steal money, they would confidently say, "By Allah, I did not do that or steal it." However, if we were to ask them to swear by the saint or by their peers that they did not steal, they would refrain out of fear—believing that if they were to swear by *al-Badawi*, or *Tijani*, or *al-Shathili*, or *Jilani*, harm will get to them or their families and hence, they can't do this. Of course this is blatant *shirk*.

STAGE OF FEAR IN THE LENS OF THE PROPHET AND HIS *ṢAḤABAH*

Stage of Fear in the Lens of the Prophet and His *Ṣaḥabah*

How did the Prophet (praise and peace of Allah be upon him) and his companions deal with the fear of Allah? Undoubtedly if we mention the Prophet's fear of Allah, it will take us hours to mention how he spent nights weeping, with tears wetting his beard and the floor. This is the Prophet of Allah—the best of Allah's creation. Someone who has a *carte blanche*—whatever he did in the past, whatever he is doing right now and whatever he will do in the future, is all forgiven. Yet, he fears Allah like this.

We, on the other hand, have nothing like him (praise and peace of Allah be upon him). Yet, we are so secure and safe from Allah's wrath and punishment that we never shed a tear except when we hear a love song or watch a sad clip or the likes! Tears do not shed from our eyes and no fear of Allah, except over issues of this materialistic life—*dunya*. This is a serious indication that our *'aqidah* is in great danger. We all have issues with the fear of Allah.

Abu Bakr (may Allah be pleased with him) used to hold his tongue and say, "This is what will take me to bad places." He (may Allah be pleased with him) feared the consequences of what he would say.

> Dawud ibn 'Ali reported: Umar ibn al-Khaṭṭab (may Allah be pleased with him), said, "If a lost sheep under my care were to die on the banks of the Euphrates, I would expect Allah the Exalted to question me about it on the Day of Resurrection."
>
> (Ḥilyat al-Awliya' 137)

This is a frightening matter for everyone who has responsibilities. Whether you are a King, a President, a parent or a manager—if you have responsibilities, Allah will ask you about everything that was under your responsibility.

Additionally, 'Umar (may Allah be pleased with him) also mentioned that "If someone from heaven were to call and say all of you are in *Jannah*, except one—I fear that I would be that one person." *SubḥānAllāh*, 'Umar (may Allah be pleased with him) feared that everyone would go to *Jannah* except him. What about us? What kind of fear do we have in our hearts?

Abu Hurayrah (may Allah be pleased with him) was narrating a hadith about the first three people who will be thrown into hellfire.

He said: "The Prophet (praise and peace of Allah be upon him) said that the first three people that will enter hellfire are…" he wept and could not continue the sentence and fainted. As he wakes up, he tries to continue but he weeps again. He fainted three times until he managed to pull himself together and narrate the hadith. He said: I heard the Messenger of Allah say: The first of men (whose case) will be decided on the Day of Judgement will be a man who died as a martyr. He shall be brought (before the Judgement Seat). Allah will make him recount His blessings (i.e. the blessings which He had bestowed upon him) and he will recount them (and admit having enjoyed them in his life). (Then) will Allah say: What did you do (to requite these blessings)? He will say: I fought for Thee until I died as a martyr. Allah will say: You have told a lie. You fought that you might be called a 'brave warrior'. And you were called so. (Then) orders will be passed against him and he will be dragged with his face downward and cast into hell. Then will be brought forward a man who acquired knowledge and imparted it (to others) and recited the Qur'an. He will be brought and Allah will make him recount His blessings and he will recount them (and admit having enjoyed them in his lifetime). Then will Allah ask:

What did you do (to requite these blessings)? He will say: I acquired knowledge and disseminated it and recited the Qur'an seeking Thy pleasure. Allah will say: You have told a lie. You acquired knowledge so that you might be called a scholar,' and you recited the Qur'an so that it might be said: 'He is a *Qari* and such has been said. Then orders will be passed against him and he shall be dragged with his face downward and cast into the Fire. Then will be brought a man whom Allah had made abundantly rich and had granted every kind of wealth. He will be brought and Allah will make him recount His blessings and he will recount them and (admit having enjoyed them in his lifetime). Allah will (then) ask: What have you done (to requite these blessings)? He will say: I spent money in every cause in which Thou wished that it should be spent. Allah will say: You are lying. You did (so) that it might be said about (You): 'He is a generous fellow' and so it was said. Then will Allah pass orders and he will be dragged with his face downward and thrown into Hell."

(Ṣaḥīḥ Muslim 1905a)

Not only that, Abu Hurayrah (may Allah be pleased with him), his wife and his slave used to get up and remain awake for one-third of the night by turns. Each would offer the night prayer and then awaken the other. Abu Hurayrah (may Allah be pleased with Him) used to divide the night into three parts:

> Abu Hurayrah (may Allah be pleased with Him), his wife and his slave used to get up and remain awake for one-third of the night by turns. Each would offer the night prayer and then awaken the other. One-third, he (may Allah be pleased with Him) will pray while they sleep. Another one-third, he (may Allah be pleased with Him) sleeps while one of the others stands to pray. For the other one-third, he (may Allah be pleased with Him) would be awake and recalling the hadith of the Prophet (praise and peace of Allah be upon him) that he had learnt and memorised from him.
>
> (Sunan al-Darimi 264)

BENEFITS OF HAVING FEAR OF ALLAH

Benefits of Having Fear of Allah

Essentially, fear highly relates to sincerity. When we fear Allah (Glory be to Him, the Exalted), we do not go around showing off to people our good deeds because we conceal such deeds so that it would be for the sake of Allah while at the same time, we are not certain whether Allah accepted them from us or not.

I once sat with an editor of one of the biggest English newspapers in the country. His newspaper was notorious for posting indecent photos of females on the last page of his publication. One day, I went to speak to him and give him advice and tell him it was haram. He said, "Shaykh, I know it is wrong but do you know how many people accepted Islam through me? Thirty-seven men and women!" What was he insinuating? He was justifying his sins by saying that he has done a lot for Allah! If he had fear of Allah, he'd be contemplating on whether his deeds were accepted or not. That would have prevented him from boasting about such deeds in the first place, let alone watering down such indecency and calling for sin publicly! Therefore, sincerity and fear go side by side.

The fear of Allah pushes us to do more good deeds and refrains us from indulging sins.

Let me give another example: I pray five *farḍ ṣalah*, however, it is not enough since I have too many sins. Hence, I will pray twelve more *rak'ah* of sunnah. But, it is still not enough. What about *ḍuḥa* prayers?

> "In the morning, charity is due on every joint bone of the body of every one of you. Every *tasbiḥah* (i.e., saying *SubḥānAllāh*) is an act of charity, and every *taḥmidah* (i.e., saying *Alḥamdulillāh*) is an act of charity and every *tahlillah* (i.e., saying *lā ʾilāha ʾillā-llāh*) is an act of charity; and enjoining *Ma'ruf* (good) is an act of charity, and forbidding *Munkar* (evil) is an act of charity, and two *rak'ah ḍuḥa* prayers which one performs in the forenoon is equal to all this (in reward)."
>
> (Riyaḍ aṣ-Ṣaliḥin 1140)

The Prophet (praise and peace of Allah be upon him) mentioned in the above hadith that the *ḍuḥa* prayer is like giving charity for the 360 joints we are due upon. Thus, if you are not praying *ḍuḥa* every day, start doing it. I only started doing it twenty-five years ago. I was a big Shaykh then, however, I did not pray *ḍuḥa*. In my school, I found a teacher who barely had a beard, but every day in his spare class, at eleven o'clock, without saying anything, he goes to take his *wuḍu'*—lay his praying mat in the teachers' room and prayed two *rak'ah*. When I saw this, I said to myself, "*Wallāhi*, shame on you. You are a Shaykh. You teach people, yet you don't do it?" Since then, he has been getting credit for every time I pray *ḍuḥa*. And he did not even open his mouth to tell me to pray. This is the beauty of *da'wah*. So pray *ḍuḥa*. *Inshā'Allāh*, I will gain credit every time you do it.

Next, the fear of Allah pushes us to do good deeds and makes us hasten to *Jannah*. The Prophet (praise and peace of Allah be upon him) said:

> "Whoever is concerned should set out when it is still night and whoever sets out when it is still night will reach the destination. Verily the merchandise of Allah is expensive, verily the merchandise of Allah is Paradise."

(Jami' at-Tirmidhi 2450)

Whoever is afraid, travels in the beginning of the night. People back then did not travel in the morning because of the heat of the sun, so they used to travel at night because it is quicker and safer when they travel. This is a metaphor; if you are afraid of the Hellfire, then you should do a lot of good deeds.

Furthermore, one of the benefits of fearing Allah is that we will be under the shade of Allah. The Prophet of

Allah said:

> "Seven people Allah will give them His Shade on the Day when there would be no shade but the Shade of His Throne (i.e., on the Day of Resurrection): And they are: a just ruler; a youth who grew up with the worship of Allah; a person whose heart is attached to the mosques, two men who love and meet each other and depart from each other for the sake of Allah; a man whom an extremely beautiful woman seduces (for illicit relation), but he (rejects this offer and) says: 'I fear Allah'; a man who gives in charity and conceals it (to such an extent) that the left-hand does not know what the right has given; and a man who remembers Allah in solitude and his eyes become tearful".
>
> (Riyaḍ aṣ-Ṣaliḥin 449)

The vast majority of the youth today will probably say, "Shaykh, where is this woman? I'm here, I'm available." This man was lured and seduced, and then he says and proclaims that he fears Allah. And so, he will be granted Allah's shade. Those who fear Allah (Glory be to Him, the Exalted) in this *dunya*, will not be afraid on the Day of Judgement. And those who are not afraid from Allah's torments in this *dunya* will be in torment on the Day of Judgement, as per the hadith below:

The prophet (praise and peace of Allah be upon him) said: "Allah, may He be glorified and exalted, says: 'By My might, I will not let My slave suffer from fear in two realms or feel safe in two realms. If he feels safe from Me in this world, I will make him feel fear on the Day of Resurrection, but if he fears Me in this world, I will make him feel safe on the Day of Resurrection.'"

(Ṣaḥīḥ ibn Hibbān 640)

HOPE

HOPE IN ALLAH

Hope in Allah

What is hope in Islam? It is *ar-Raja'*. *Ar-Raja'* is when our heart is connected to Allah (Glory be to Him, the Exalted). We are feeling happy and optimistic of Allah's favour and blessings coming over us. We are feeling the peace and tranquillity in our hearts because we know who Allah is. It is the total opposite of fear.

For example, when we hold our one-year-old child, and toss them in the air, what do they do? They laugh and enjoy it. In a similar manner, with Allah being the highest example, those who have hope in Allah feel like a child being tossed in the air. They know that Allah will catch them—that Allah will forgive them, that Allah will grant them *Jannah*.

For whom did Allah make *Jannah* for? For you and me—for us. All we have to do is think positively of Allah (Glory be to Him, the Exalted) and do what He commanded us to do and refrain from what He had prohibited.

AR-RAJA' AND *TAMANNI*
(BEING HOPEFUL VS BEING WISHFUL)

Ar-Raja' and Tamanni (Being Hopeful vs Being Wishful)

What is the difference between being hopeful—*ar-Raja'*—and being wishful—*tamanni*? Being wishful is when we are lazy and commit many sins yet still have the audacity to say: "I will open the door for the Prophet (praise and peace of Allah be upon him) to *Jannah* from the inside." This means that we believe that we will enter Jannah before the Prophet (praise and peace of Allah be upon him). This is nonsense—and this is being wishful.

On the other hand, being hopeful is, for example, when we observe our *fard* prayers in the *masjid*, we pray the night prayers every night, we do good deeds, we read the Qur'an once every month at least, we give charity and we avoid all major and minor sins—and are hopeful that Allah accepts our deeds.

ATTAINING
AR-RAJA'

Attaining *Ar-Raja'*

How can we attain this level of hopefulness in Allah (Glory be to Him, the Exalted)? By looking at Allah's previous favours and blessings upon us.

Has Allah given us all what we had ever wanted even without asking Him? Of course! We can stand, speak, see, eat, and move around and this is only by the will and blessing of Allah alone without us deserving it. These are all favours from Allah. Hence, this should make us feel hopeful in Allah's continuous gifts and blessings, and that He does not let us down. He (Glory be to Him, the Exalted) will continue to give us blessings from means we do not anticipate.

Furthermore, we should bear in mind the promise of Allah on *Jannah* when we read the Qur'an and the sunnah. What has Allah promised us? A lot of beautiful things. Whenever we come across verses of *Jannah*, and see what is in it, our heart will fly and say, "I will be there, I am one of the inhabitants of *Jannah*, with the grace of Allah, I know that." In a nutshell, the beautiful verses of *Jannah* will make us hope and *du'a'* to Allah to allow us to be among the people of *Jannah*.

We should also recognise Allah's continuous favours and blessings upon us. Many of us are blessed with a house, children, spouse, wealth and more. Not only that, Allah also has bestowed plenty of His other blessings upon us without us asking for it! Think about this. Are all the things that you have been given to you because you asked for it? Did you ask Allah to give you each and every one of the things that you have currently? NO. Allah gives us without us asking for it, but we never appreciate that.

Among other things that helps us to be hopeful is remembering Allah's forgiveness. Allah's forgiveness is beyond imagination. And this is why the more we study Allah's beautiful names, the more we love Allah, and the more we become hopeful.

al-Karīm: *The Most Generous.*

ar-Rahīm: *The Most Merciful.*

al-Ghaffār: *The One who Forgives.*

al-Jawad: *The One that Gives.*

at-Tawwāb: *The One who guides people to repent and then accepts Repentance.*

"Four persons would be brought out from the Fire and would be presented to Allah. One of them would turn (towards the He s.w.t) and say: 'O' my Lord, when Thou hast brought me out from it, do not throw me back into it', and Allah would rescue him from it."

(Ṣaḥiḥ Muslim 192)

"I heard the Prophet (praise and peace of Allah be upon him) saying, 'If somebody commits a sin and then says, 'O' my Lord! I have sinned, please forgive me!' and his Lord says, 'My slave has known that he has a Lord who forgives sins and punishes for it, I therefore have forgiven my slave (his sins).' Then he remains without committing any sin for a while and then again commits another sin and says, 'O' my Lord, I have committed another sin, please forgive me,' and Allah says, 'My slave has known that he has a Lord who forgives sins and punishes for it, I, therefore, have forgiven my slave (his sin).' Then he remains without Committing another sin for a while and then commits another sin (for the third time) and says, 'O' my Lord, I have committed another sin, please forgive me,' and Allah says, 'My slave has known that he has a Lord Who forgives sins and punishes for it I therefore have forgiven My slave (his sin), he can do whatever he likes.'"

(Ṣaḥiḥ al-Bukhari 7507)

What does this mean? Does it mean that we should go and commit sin? No, of course not. It means that as long as we sin because of our human nature, our weakness—and we repent and feel remorseful in our hearts, and ask for Allah's forgiveness, Allah will forgive us regardless of how big our sins are. Allah will forgive us regardless of how many times we do it. Allah will forgive us as long as we fulfil the conditions of repentance.

BENEFITS OF HAVING HOPE IN ALLAH

Benefits of Having Hope in Allah

What are the benefits of having hope—*ar-raja'* in Allah?

1. One of the main benefits of having hope in Allah is that it is the main reason that will help us in finding the sweetness of *iman*, and forms of worship.

   Have you thought about why some of us look so grumpy when they pray? Why do we think of worldly matters while praying and then complain about not finding the sweetness of *ṣalah*? It is because we do not have hope in Allah. We are sceptical and pessimistic of Allah. We pray without knowing if Allah accepts it or not. We pray just to get it off our chest, off our backs. However, when we have great hope in Allah, our *ʿibadah* has a special sweetness to it.

2. It expresses our *ubudiyyah* (obedience).

   Having hope in Allah expresses our *ubudiyyah* as a slave when we make *duʿa'*. If we hope for something, we will not be able to attain it without *duʿa'*, and hence should make lots of it. Consequently, making lots of *duʿa'* will help us escape the wrath of Allah as we ask Him for protection.

BALANCING AL-KHAWF WA RAJA'

Balancing *Al-khawf Wa Raja'*

It is extremely important to strike a balance between the fear and hope in Allah. Why? Because for us—*Ahlus Sunnah wal Jama'ah*—we believe that we are distinct from the seventy-two deviant sects destined for Hell, since only one will be in *Jannah* as the Prophet (praise and peace of Allah be upon him) said. And they are those who align themselves with the Prophet's (praise and peace of Allah be upon him) teachings and those of his companions.

Our belief underscores that *iman* can both increase and decrease—growing with good deeds and decreasing with sins. The *Khawarij* and the *Murji'ah* hold contrasting views. The *Khawarij* assert that committing a major sin causes the whole *iman* to be gone; rendering one a *kafir*. This extreme stance leads to excessive fear; a single lie or act of theft for example, could brand one a *kafir*.

Conversely, the *Murji'ah*, unfortunately, the predominant among Muslims today, adopt a lax approach. They argue that as long as one maintains *iman* and *taqwa*—we can party all night long, drink booze, do drugs, lie, cheat, do *riba'* and more. They say we can do all those things and that all we have to say is *lā ĭlāha ĭllā-llāh*, and we can enter *Jannah*. In essence, they are saying that our *iman* can never decrease.

However, *Ahlus Sunnah wal Jama'ah* emphasises a balanced approach. They link fear and hope to the wings of a bird— if one is stronger than the other, then the bird will tilt and fall. However both equally being strong will allow the bird to fly. This analogy resonates with the Qur'an:

> "On the Day [some] faces will turn white and [some] faces will turn black…"
>
> (Ali-'Imran, 3:106)

Allah also mentioned in the Qur'an:

> "…Indeed, your Lord is swift in penalty; but indeed, He is Forgiving and Merciful."
>
> (al-A'raf 7:167)

Therefore, let it be known that every fear of Allah must have hope, and every hope in Allah, must have fear. If our fear does not have any hope, it will despair us from Allah's mercy, and this will take us to Hell. On the other hand, if our hope is without fear, we will indulge in doing sin without worrying about anything else due to having such high hopes in Allah, and that will lead us to Hell as well.

DISTINGUISHING MOMENTS OF FLUCTUATING HOPE AND FEAR

Distinguishing Moments of Fluctuating Hope and Fear

Hope and fear, though they have to be balanced, at times one must exceed the other. For example, at the time of death—when we are dying, what is the best thing to do? Is it to fear Allah more or to be hopeful of Allah more?

The answer is: one must be hopeful of Allah. We must have hope exceeding our fear in that state of being on our deathbed. This is because fear pushes us to do good deeds, but on our dying bed, we cannot do anything other than to be hopeful in Allah's mercy! The only thing you have is this straw (hope) that you have to hang onto in this ocean (death). Hence, the only thing we must do is to think positively of Allah—which is why most people during the time of their death would ask others to remind them of their good deeds as it gives them hope in Allah. The Prophet (praise and peace of Allah be upon him) mentioned in the following hadith:

None of you should die but hoping only good from Allah, the Exalted and Glorious."

(Ṣaḥīḥ Muslim 2877c)

This is an instruction: When we are on our deathbed, we must have hope in Allah and think well of Him.

Consequently, in cases where we should make fear more prevalent—for example, when we are in the state of security—being safe and secure. When people feel secure in their lavish homes, with their healthy children, massive amounts of money in their bank, and their successful business—they must be fearful of Allah. Why? Because when we are secure, *shaytan* is actually preparing to strike us hard. He is marinating us like a good chef, waiting for the right moment to lead us astray and be forgetful of Allah. Hence, we need to become fearful of Allah during the times we are secure as well, as the Prophets and Messengers used to fear Allah then as well.

Additionally, we must also have fear exceeding and prevailing our hopes when we are sinning. When we listen to music or watch haram movies, some would do *istighfar*. Meaning, while they are watching the haram, they are saying *istighfar*—this is making fun of Allah. Why? Is *istighfar* haram? Of course not! However, in this situation, you must fear Allah and refrain from doing haram!

Furthermore, whenever we feel safe and secure, feeling confident that we will enter into Paradise, we must make fear prevail.

> Imam Aḥmad Bin Hanbal was asked: "When does a servant truly taste the joy of rest?" He replied: "When the first foot enters *Jannah* (Paradise)"
>
> (Tabaqat Al Hanabila 1/293)

Before we put our foot in Paradise—we will never be safe, we will never be comfortable. It will always be agony, torment, and trials from Allah. However, the moment we put our first foot in *Jannah*, no one is going to take us out of it. We are there to stay. This is when our eternal comfort and safety will be achieved—by praying to Allah that He makes us among the inhabitants of *Jannah*, and that He puts in our hearts the fear of Him, the hope in what He has for us, and to be balanced as per the way of *Ahlus Sunnah wal Jama'ah*, the saved group.

www.ingramcontent.com/pod-product-compliance
Lightning Source LLC
LaVergne TN
LVHW061622070526
838199LV00078B/7384